EXOTIC DANCING OF THE SOUL

EXOTIC DANCING OF THE SOUL

By

Lin Forest

ISBN 1-58721-181-5

1stbooks – rev. 2/10/00

ABOUT THE BOOK

Exotic Dancing of the Soul is a collection of intimate poetry that spans the author's lifetime and was inspired by its story. The story includes love, passion, discovery, spiritual awakening, sadness, disappointment, anger and despair. Each feeling is shared in the journey backward to the dark times. Through poetry, or "playing with words", the victory of spirit emerges from a survivor of abuse, rape and cancer. This bumpy road to the metamorphosis of the soul is best described in the poem, "The Grind", from which the title of the book is derived.

The style of the 124 poems in the book is brief, direct and unburdened by convention. Line breaks and lengths contribute to the feeling of each selection that can range from passionate longing to hardened cynicism. The poetry is refreshing, taking full advantage of

"License
To cross the boundaries
Without looking back
For commas…"

Special thanks to Cindy Dollard, Anytime Arts for Cover Artwork

Dedication

*To S. Michael and Michael S. and all of the Angels who have
gone Between
To Aaron and Miriam
And to Tomorrow*

Table of Contents

POETIC ANTICIPATION

My pen swells
Words too big
It seems
To lie down
On the sheets
Without encouragement
Caresses and a kiss
For luck
Or some such endearment
Anything
For the creative merging
Of word to word
Vow to vow
License
To cross the boundaries
Without looking back
For commas

IT HAS BEEN LIFE

I tell only
Of air
And breathing
Of mountains
And climbing
Of creatures
Of clouds
And flying
Of water
Seas
Wet stuff
And wind
Molecules
And organs
Moon, stars
And sun
And being
Inside
One another
The journey
There
And back
All you need
Really
It has been
Life

SOUL-MATE

I touch you
Without touching,
Inches apart
Or miles,
I feel your
Light heat
Merge with mine,
And, rising,
I pass through
You, aglow.
Comet's tail,
You'll come around
Again.

TIME IN THE BOTTLE

I remember
A blonde lover
I'd known before
The years left
One by one
Sometimes breaking line
And running
By me
Barely seen
Leaving me
Alone with memory
Of his long hair
On my thighs
And wet grass
Held tightly
Even the smells
Drift up
Historic preservation
Bottled memory
Cold glass

NOT COFFEE

My heart drips,
Turned upside down,
Thick dark bits
Of forgotten ground
At the bottom,
The beginning,
Now to be emptied.
Awakening demands
A fresh-filled cup
Held in shaking hands.
Sun coming up.

CANDLE

I run my fingers
Through the flame
Just to feel the burn
Start eating my flesh
Like putting my hand
On your warm neck
Fingers crawl into your hair
And there's fire
Everywhere I touch you
An altar filled with prayers
Candle lights
Fireworks pre-show
Pyrotechnic temptation

THE AIR I BREATHE

Your lips
That mouth
Touching me
You take
My breath
Away
Drawn
Into you
Leaving me
Willingly
Emptied
I ache
To remain
Inside you
But requisite
Inhalation
And you're
Filling me
With all
The two of us
Have lost
Together
We breathe
Fresh air

TO SWIM WITH THE DOLPHIN

I remember you now
The waves gray and white
Wind-tickled and moving
In and out
As I walked
Looking at cloud wisps
And seagulls gliding
To kiss the possibility
Of each wet tip
Then you came
Dark mystery rising
In and out
Of the wintry sea
And we went together
Along the boundary
Of my world
And of yours
And I marveled then
That you continued
Beside me silent
Not touching
Dolphin wisdom
I suppose

KNOWING ME

When you touch
You go very deep
Fingers soft
Persistent
You touch heart
And keep on
Going
Rubbing nerves
Knowing
To the core
Vertebrae
You touch hard
Reaching
Through me
Going where
Others
Never dared
Never cared
And I am
Known

COMMUNIQUÉ

I wanted you
All day long
Sent you lines
Of love thoughts
As wet as me
Waiting for you
On those stairs
Those long legs
Taking two
At a time
And bare against
Me hard inside
No words
Just your legs
Rubbing mine
Like cricket songs
Message received

ONE-TWO-TWO-THREE

No one does the magic
Like you
Never did
Understand the blue
Aura spirit breath of love
You fill me
When I open more
You're there too
Demanding to be forgotten
In another time
I would love you more
But there are no words
Inside me
You've touched them all
Hand-dexed
I've been known
Well
Again
You fill me.
One…

INTIMATE INSIGHTS

When you open me up
And swear you see
Right through me
Incision up the center
Between the ribs
Cut to the heart
Still beating pumping
Your eyes are the mirrors
Alien autopsy
You see me gray
Too strange to hold
Without gloves

GRETEL

You slip away
Just when I think
I've got you
Figured out
Again.

Gretel, I go on
Following the crumbs
You drop, one by one
Bits of yourself
Clues.

I follow each
Until I lose you
In deeper forest.
Who are you
Anyway?

You keep me hungry
Picking up bits
Nibbling at knowing you
Starving me
Slowly.

But I'll find you
Someday, some night
When you're not
Expecting me
To feast.

MIDNIGHT

There are black eyes
In my nights now,
Ebony on shadow,
Subtle enriching.
That's how you fill me,
Weave yourself into me.

I close my eyes,
And you're still there.
I feel your breathing
On my face, hair,
The smell of your hands,
And I know you.

Skin barriers fade.
I want to be inside you,
Basic body greed
To share breathing,
Heart beating,
Swimming through you.

But it is not enough.
Dark slips away from day.
Always sun rising,
Light daggers
Between us,
Night hungry always.

THE CIRCLE

I recognized you
Felt you
Inside me
Behind me
Past lives
Together
Or a shadow.
I can never
Quite spin round
Fast enough
To catch you.
Maybe
Next time.

SOMETIMES I LOVE YOU FOREVER

Sometimes I love you so hard
I want to scream,
Primal rebellion at the space,
Distance between us,
The illogic of oneness
Split by the physiological.

Sometimes I love you so quietly
I awaken to find you
Curled up inside me warmly,
Cherished, held gently,
All the comfort and nurturing
Of fireside dreams and holding.

Sometimes I love you forever
Or know that I have and will,
Half remember other journeys,
Nights passed in loving,
Years racing behind us
And before us,
Breaths mingled past separation.

TWO AND A.M.

This night is deep
It's two
Me and you
This a.m.
Me piling up pillows
You off somewhere
Doing what men do
With empty beside them.
And horizon out front
And I'm just pretending
My legs could hold you.

JUST SO

I want to lie
Just so
Stretch my feet out
Beside yours and find
Mine smaller

I want to hear your heart
Through my hand laid
Gently to rest
Just there
Where the breathing surrounds
And hums the rhythm
Of your almost sleeping
Next to me

I want to turn and curl
And find you've matched
The shape
Just so
Filling in all the holes
And breathing out
As I breathe in
Your promised
Immortality

MAY-EMBER INTERLUDE

You wonder, ponder about
The nature, character of this
Enchantment you've uncovered,
The flames licking at your heart,
Pain creeping up beneath
A warmth you can't resist.

Green wood, your heart, young.
In too many ways you burn,
Crack, sizzle, smoking up tears.
I had forgotten the crackling
And the hardness inside my chest,
Coals I thought too cold to turn.

You poke and push embers,
Dangerous sparks flying about.
And we burn, raging, loving,
Hurting more than you thought
Matches of this type ever could.

Charred, scarred, hearts melting,
Memories like ash in the wind,
Romantic interlude ending,
A draft, flue closed.
Someone else is going to bed.

H$_2$0

My world is wet
Wet sex
Wet birth
Wet blood
And tears
Bays and
Rivers
Oceans
Drops
My fingers drip
Wet words
Ached up from
The gut
Liver
Heart
Tears
To know
I am alive.

But life with you
Was dry
So dry
All cried out
Dry-birthed
And aborted
Bled near death
And dry
Dried up
Cracked
Ready to blow
Away in the wind
Until
The storm.

IN MY HAIR

I like the smell of you
Always, not just after
Scrubbing and soaking
And powder dust storms
But the really you
The one I recognized
The first time you
Breathed into
My hair
Every strand
Alive with
Your singularity
Your only oneness
Uniqueness
Completeness
And you are
Still there

122

The last time
You touched me
Not knowing
It was the last time
Touching
We held
The path
Between hearts
And lips
Kissing hands.
Goodbyes
Always break
One
Into
Two.

To
One
We had been
Reunited
From the pieces.
We were only parts
Memory wisps
Until molecules
Electrons, energy
Flowing between us
Touching.
They still know
The way
From two
To
One.

THE CALL

Then I will go to North Africa,
Sit in the desert,
Eat sand,
Spit sand,
Sleep sand,
And write,
Write sand, too,
To you.
And when I return,
Sanded down,
Brown and smooth,
Worn down,
New groove,
Will you want me
For the journey?
For the having been there,
Vicarious trek
Through sand and storm
And not having you for so long?
For then you will not fit
Me any longer.
I will be African desert
No man can fill,
Too warmed by the sand and sun
To need your thin arms
Around me
Anymore.

BONDING

Men suck
The love
Right out
Of me
Walking away
Super-magnets
Pulling buttons
Off my
Shirt, pants
All the steel
Of good
Intentions
Aorta ripped
Right out, too
Squirting
Life juice
All over
Me turning
Inside out
Again damn
Intimacy
Super glue
To put me
Back together

NIGHT WALKER

I want you always,
Even when the clouds drip rain for days,
And fog crawls along the streets,
Engulfing, digesting, unsuspecting pedestrians.

But I know you want yourself, too,
And are wandering about
In the puddles and white darkness,
Hunting for who you are
And where you've missed
Finding yourself.

TO ARTHUR OR JAMES
AND CHARLES

I have red pubic hair,
Thighs which ripple when
They aren't supposed to,
Long toes that I like to use.
I hate wearing shoes.
I am young at forty-two,
Feeling very old and wise,
Finding new things with surprise.
I am forgiving now of those
Who mispronounce my name
When they call.
There aren't very many
Anymore,
But I go on searching for
Someone to make my bed
And bring me flowers
On Tuesdays and Halloween.
I am just myself and I have seen
The mountains when they were highest,
And I am most sorry now
For the ice cream cones I forewent
And the nights I did not kiss you.

GUARDING ME

I saw the image
Just a possibility
Pistol firing at my head
But you flinched
Before I did
Ricochet thought bullets
Red filling your eyes
Before mine opened
My mirror
Lover
You're too tight
Around my throat
Honey to let
Me stop breathing
Safety always on
With you

OTHER LOVE STORIES

I am tired of reading
Other poets' poetry,
Exasperated with media
Portrayals of love found,
Mouths kissed, commercials
About getting what we
Think we see.

I was tired yesterday when
Two mouths found each other
In the park on the bridge
I was crossing over.

I was tired and frowning,
And the mouths ignored me.
And tonight I will cry
Wet pillows and sheets.

I am tired of sleeping without you,
Trying to remember how
Your legs wrapped around mine,
And I complained in your closeness.

MOUNTAIN OWL

It's midnight
And you're where you are
Rowing hard
To get where
You never chose
To go
Up hill
Dry bed
Rocky
And a full canoe.

I spread my wings
And glide
Through the night
Meal flight
And full moon
For the inspiration
Exhalation
Following you
Unexpected
Night watchman.

I see you
Pull to the top
Again
And again
As much
For the climb
As the peak.

I sit in
The branches
And watch you
Golden eyes

Glowing
Knowing
The stream flows
Downhill.

TWILIGHT

You are nothing
But glass to me
Now I see through
And through
Your beautiful marble eyes
Your crystal ribs
And clear heart reflecting
Light and dew tears
Fallen sundrops saddened
At the coming night
Shadows pulling down
The vision perfected
At the last moment

EMERGENCE

Life with you was heavy
Always raining
Those brocade curtains
Left down across the day
Saddle oxfords
And pea coats
And knit caps in May
And we never ever
Breathed together
Not once
In forty-five years
The air so thick
Between us
That I couldn't
See your face

But I am lighter now
Drifting up from the earth
Like mist rising
Foggy morn-break
After sleeping too long
Lifting veils
A curtain drawn
Following the light
Sun rising

NOT NOW

Alone now
There is
The thought
To die
Without you
But
Feet stick
Straight out
Denial
To the bones
So
I'll wait
Till you
Come back
Immortality
By declaration

YIN

A circle
A hole
A void
A window
Soul's eye
Empty
Or waiting.

Holes are for filling
Or passing through
Gateways
Energy paths
Or open cups
Opportunities.

Half-circle
Half-filled
I await you.

THE GRIND

My back hurts
Angel wings
Trying to grow
Flying and things
Metamorphosis
Or just
Exotic dancing
Of the soul

VEILS

I wear a veil.
You would not know me.
Only the eyes tell.
I keep them closed
When you watch me,
Lashes the forest
You must pass through
On your journey
To my heart
Through pale lashes,
Pale eyes,
Body disguise.

ATTRIBUTION

The heat in my hands
Is not mine
But You
Pouring through me
As always
You surround me
Hold me
Let me lean
Against You
Awhile
As You warm
My heart
As always

911

The siren
Ambulance
Or Rescue
Screeching
Shrieking
Racing nearer
Nearer
Then farther
Farther
Pumping
To bring
Someone back
From the Edge
Someone who might
Just Fall

Then the quiet
No siren
No fear
Of the Night
Someone gliding
With their own
Wings
Rescue
Achieved

GOING UP

I take
My clothes
Off and
Run quite
Naked
Upstairs
And down,
And up
Again,
Birthing
Canal
Practice
Reversed,
Hold my
Breath and
Push now,
Last time,
I swear:
Dying
Without
Midwife.

MEETING JOE

As much as Death is feared,
He is embraced.
The blinding white light
Is only love-energy
Released,
As are you.
The corpse is stricken
Still with wonder
Released,
And smiles.
Fear not.

CLIMAX

Joy
Light
Bright
Warm
Expanding
Pulled in
No fear
Orgasm
Of the soul
Forever
Going
Outward
Into the universe.

Who would have
Thought?
Seen?
Felt?
Known?
Gone?
Without
The death
Angel
Dark
Seductress?

3 WISHES

To be happy with
Whatever you get.
To be happy with
However long you have.
To be happy with
Whomever you are happy
With.
Connected
Head to heart
Crown to ground.
Reverse the flow
Heart to head
Ground to crown
And beyond.
You can fly
Happy with.
With:
The answer.

OLD EYES

When I hold your face
In the center of my True Eye,
I see two –
The eyes of an Old One,
The mouth of Youth.
You smile and laugh,
Swim with that tongue
Diving for word-pearls,
In the coldest Sea
While deep eyes watch
Over years and tears
From the Mountains
Your Spirit has climbed.
Nearness to the Sun
Has weathered the Eye,
But together, Youth and Age,
You dance
Life's Circle of One,
Still smiling,
Still crying,
One breath
At a time.

THE SOARING SOUL

The butterfly
Is invisible,
Emergent
From life,
Nothingness
Too free to
Capture
In flight.

THE CLEARING

I saw
A white dress
Red flowers
Drop by drop
Head emptied
Clear at last
From inside out
Goodbye said
Hello meant
Butterfly flown
Cracked cocoon

ICARUS

I am passion
Contained.
I am compassion
Unrestrained.
I am the air
Thinned
Too near
The sun.
Icarus knew
The falling.
Couldn't hold onto
His wings
Either.

UNSHRINKING

Alone
Lone
One.
No
Shrinking.

Withdrawing
Detaching
Pruning
Only
To grow wide.

Once through the door
Expand
Disperse
Explode
Into the Light.

One star
Lone journey
Before nova
Death's funnel
Upside down.

TUTELAGE

I am born
Again and again,
Beginning
And ending
The same lessons
Over and over:
Divine remediation.

OUT OF BODY

I saw you through
My closed eyes,
Dream walking,
Unnoticed intrusion.
We are more alive when
No one is watching.
I touched you then
Without fear,
Braver when
No one is watching.
The corpse
Without the wake,
I lie here,
Wandering prematurely.

NEXT GENERATION

The sun in
Her black eyes
She speaks of
Good mother
Father still
I watch her
Mouth moving
No sound scrapes
My empty
Heart drum shell
Tree fallen
Years ago
Roots pulled up
Eaten out
Returning
To the earth
Bad to good
Dead to life
Try again
Lazarus wood

INEVITABILITY

I'm going to die
Damn
Know I will too
Damn
Young to be old
Damn
Enough to know
Damn
Better than to
Damn
Trust the sunrise
Damn
It doesn't some
Damn
Times

NOT SIMPLE

Simple wants
Less pain
More joy
A few more years
To watch my
Children grow
To not know when
I'm dying
To find someone
To hold my hand
Look into my eyes
And forget the commas
Questions periods
No punctuation
Or stop and go
Forward only
One moment at a time
Time as one moment
After another
Only
Simple wants

THE FALLING TREE

The sound
Of one hand
Clapping
Is the
Expectation
Of another.
To sing
Alone,
Hearing
Harmony.
The forest is full.

RAINBOW METAPHYSICS
AND CHAKRA DANCE

Blues and
Yellows
Greens
Where Blue
Touches
Yellow
Spirit
To Body
Touching
Me
To the Heart.
We Dance.

WITH EYES CLOSED

Looking for peace
In the back of my mind,
Filling the glass
By drinking the wine.

My journey is longer
The more that I seek.
Answers are questions
We write with our feet.

Walking in shadows,
Unlit candles for light,
Peace in the Eye's opening,
Not in the sight.

CONQUEST

Self-knowledge,
No matter how
You get it,
Artery or
Vein,
Hurts.

I ache with the wounds,
Life's Truth-droplets,
Falling like shrapnel
Straight through my chest,
Ready-made pinholes
For the pinning on
Of medals
Won in the conquest
Of Self.

CHARMIAN KARMA CIRCLE

Karma is Karma
That is all
The circle
Is a Snake
Bending back
Touching itself
In surprise
Electric
Joy-pain
It closes
And is One
Again
As always
We roll on

COURAGE

When waves of fear
Wash over you,
Rest on the beach.

When fear rains
Down upon you,
Be cleansed.

The fountain of your fear
Falls from the river
Of your soul.

So you may rest by the water,
Knowing it is your own.

EVOLUTION

As the pendulum swings
Each of us journeys
From frontier to frontier
Finding our limits
The rhythm of growth
Seeking the balance
The middle way

Some pendulums fly
Silver and crystal
They swing wider, harder
Violently crashing, breaking
Against both walls
But in the pieces, fragments
Of themselves on the floor
Diamond chips sparkle, glint
In new sunlight's rays

FROM THE DOVES (in gratitude)

Loved one,
Divine alchemist,
Turning hearts
Into gold.
You are the catalyst,
Metamorphic guide,
Making shadows
Into wings.
We fly.

HAND

I want you to save me.
Reach out, take my hand,
Pull me from the flames
And stay with me on the rocks
Until I'm strong enough to stand.

I don't require a miracle.
Just a touch will do,
For I've been here a long, long time,
Burning, suffering, being strengthened,
Waiting for the healing that is you.

CARTOON HOMECOMING

After all,
Lonely woman child,
Father, mother, home erased.
Little Orphan Annie,
Holes for eyes.
No windows,
Mirrors
Of the erasure.

You can fall into them, those eyes,
Fall all the way down to her heart.
A dive, a fall, or just a wrong turn,
And you're there.
Click your heels three times,
And you're still there.
Heart is where the home is,
After all.

INTROSPECTIVE GLANCE

Walking by today,
I saw that my plant,
That prickly cactus-thing,
Has flowers now.
It's still growing.
It sucks in sun
Through the window
I put it behind
And gets by with
Only a few drops
Of wet stuff
Now and then.
I never noticed
The flowers
When I was inside
Myself,
But it smiles
At me looking in
From somewhere else.

IN THE DASH (1953 -   )

To be touched, to touch,
To be one
Even for the moment,
Defying all boundaries,
Goes beyond this world,
This time, this being,
To a unity deeper than
Any explaining on this side.
It is the 2nd Act of Life,
The dash between
Beginning and ending,
And summarizes all the striving
In between
To return to either.

We are never more real,
More alive,
And more than alive,
Than in that momentary
Sharing of broken boundaries,
Boundaries between souls,
Between bodies, between
Hearts-minds, between
Times, between
Shoulds-woulds-coulds,
With life striving to reunite
With itself.

Only the merging transcends.

IN SPITE OF ALL

I have no one on the sidelines
Cheering me onward
To ever greater exhibitions of excellence.
No one to applaud my dragons conquered
And windmills slain.
No soothing songs and touch
When I lie fallen on the field of endeavor.
None to reassure me of another fight
Which might, perhaps, be won.
None to share that victory or defeat.
No spectators at all, it seems,
But the small shadow of a man
Who once told me: all
Is the only goal worth having,
The best the only acceptable remuneration
For the battle's efforts,
Not risking failure
In reaching the greatest heights
A terrible defeat in itself.
And, in the loneliest nights in the arena,
His voice shouts out above the crowd.
One man's shadow my Sancho
As I travel ever onward
In spite of all.

JOAN-TO-BE

being strong and
not hurting and
losing by giving
in too soon I
want to be an
ark holding all
the strong I've
ever thought about
not holding on-
to a real Joan
of Ark someone
who rides out to
battle with silver
armor blessed by
someone important I
want to be a
modern-day fleur-
de-lis but they
burned Joan also
trying to find
a way to die
that will leave my
heart in the ashes

SEVEN ROOMS AND SEVEN COLORS

Seven rooms
Seven colors
A breath
For each
A breeze
To part
The veils
To free
The lights
Float beyond
The nights
Red
Orange
Yellow
Green
Blue
Indigo
And a thousand
Violet petals
Each a dream
Woven
In tomorrow
Merely glimpsed
Today

THE QUIET ONES

You can never tell.
"Is she alive?"
They ask when I am quiet.
Living, I smile.
With closed eyes, I see.

Words, the mind, things,
Merely foreplay.
In stillness I explode,
Nova of the soul.
You can never tell.

OWLS

I like owls,
Fuzzy, round, warm, cuddly,
With talons and eyes,
Sharp and sharp,
And heads that turn
Farther than you expect,
Eyes that see both sides.
That's the wisdom:
For observation
In the dark.
Who?

YOUR HARVEST MOON

Full
Orange
Moon
Burning
Hole
In the
Night
Flame
Warming
Showing
The way
Through
Dry grass
No dew
Not
A drop
Light
Without
Mercy
Your
Harvest
Single
Sight

WRESTLING FOR PENNIES

God, in omniscience,
Mercy too cruel to fathom,
Took you from me for
I would not give you up.
I go to the mat every time,
No contest, supplication:
Divine intervention
By the bell.

YANG

All my energy folds,
Half igniting,
Half blanketing,
The light.
And there's smoke,
Enough to obscure
The sight
Or send signals
Pillowing up like clouds.

Differences collide,
A spark from the flint,
Rhythm of opposites,
Of partners,
Halves,
Folded,
Energy onto itself,
Kneading:
The essence
Of the explosion.

One hand
Cannot clap.

WORDS

She held a knife
A tool, she said
Like words
Tools
For communication
Sharing
Exchanging
Merging meanings

Hold a knife
Too long
Too tightly
In the wrong place
Blood drips down
The pain goes on
A long time

With the heart's eye
See it set free
Given to the wind
The right time
The right place
Crimson butterfly
Lifted up and soaring
Those words
With wings

BESIEGED

Once there were stones,
Solid, hard,
Found, stacked up,
For privacy,
For defense,
To cover the softness,
To survive.

They worked
So well that
They became bricks,
Self-made and sealed
With mortar of tears,
Unshed.

The best of walls
To surround me,
Contain me.
Higher, higher,
Deeper, deeper,
It grew after each assault.

I look at the sky
No longer.
Now encircled,
I circle.
I am the wall.

PREMATURE EXCLAMATION

You said it was
Meant to be.
Intention
Or Destiny?
Or not
To be
At all?

Fate sits
In shadow,
Shroud
Unsewn,
Stone
Uncarved,
Your printed
Eulogy
Premature.

THE WINK

I never wanted an open coffin
But no one would believe me dead
Just run off again somewhere
Changing my name and
Dyeing my head.

Reality is the best of mothers
Always there for us
If we look closely
And never, ever believing
Our tales of living
Forever.

So touch me when I'm cold
Some satisfaction in the real.
My glee will be in touching back
With a wink
Then when I can get
Away with it.

JUNGLE SOUNDS AND NIGHT

My ears are big.
I heard Yesterday
Over and over
Still dark and loud
Thunder moving
Farther and farther
Still within the night cloud –
Until I closed
One ear.

I listen loud.
I heard Tomorrow
Over and over
Still not shining
Rainbow waiting
Farther and farther
But still just designing –
Until I closed
The other ear.

And now I hear.
This Moment only
Louder and louder
Closer and closer
Dew-cup for
The drinking
Requited –
Until I close
Both eyes.

FAITH

The little girl
Raises a hand
Pleading for help
And does not feel
The angel draw her up
Out of the body
Which anchored her
In pain
Heart crushing despair.

But she reaches out
Again
And again
Over the years
Waiting for the Answer
White wings
A halo and harp
In the silent lonely.

This is Faith
Reaching out
Until you feel
The heat of the Hand
Holding you
Still
Without
A sound
No words
No strings.

BLACK BIRD

I had been stomping again
Crushing daisies
Not hearing cries
Nature's weeping
Carnivores' gnashing
Slashing
Devouring
Hearts hardening
Far beyond arteries
Down to the bone

And he came
Flew into my life
Directly
Diving
Right into
The glass
Head on collision
Messenger
Killed
But not instantly
Crushed and
Bleeding lying
Emptied
On the ground
One large black eye
Looking up at me
A question
No answer
Expected
He forgave

SUPPLICATING

I've never reached up
Well
Not since seven
Hell
Never could trust
More
Than some heaven
Door
Not a real hand
To open
To me
God
The father

THE BLACK OR WHITE CAT

Fact stated,
Parameters set,
Must always exclude
A portion of truth,
Thesis incomplete
With fences cutting across
Its tail out there
Somewhere.
Misconception inherent
In attempting perception.
A miracle we manage
To communicate at all.

MIDDLE AND 55

There are no words
For the truly good
The horribly bad
The very ugly.
The extremes fade
Since we cannot
Fully describe them.
So they continue
To surprise us
As we commute
Along the middle,
Double-lines and
Double-nickels,
Bifocals and
Speed limits and
Mid-life middles.

NAMELESS

A name is just
What people say
When they mean you.
It is a way
Of touching,
An attempt
At reaching out.

Name me,
And I am drawn to you
But reminded
Of our separation,
Otherness,
Boundaries.
But when you
Touch me
With your hands,
Your breath,
Your heart,
There is no boundary
Between what matters.

And we exchange matter,
Molecule by molecule,
And energy flows
Between us because
It still knows the way.

FROM THE OVAL ROOM

He's going to declare war, they say.
I don't care.
A formal declaration just makes
Death a white-tie affair.

I always preferred
Informal dying myself.

But I guess the bigger jokes
Need even more profound punch lines.

NAKED

Naked,
It seems so silly
To argue about wallpaper
Or taking out the garbage.
It's rather sad, isn't it?
People can only be themselves
When there's nothing
To hide behind.

Can you imagine diplomats,
Naked,
Arguing about national superiorities?

Perhaps
That's the answer to war and peace:
Conduct the Paris Peace Talks
In the raw.

ONLY A MOAN

It was only a moan
Too quiet to heed
Some child or animal's
Broken wing to bleed
A drop or two, a sigh
Nothing more
The sacrifice, lost flight
The closing of a door
Someone on the outside
Always someone in
Only a tiny moment
Between lovers, friends
But it was only a cry
A feeble one that might
Still have opened the door
For that angel's
Untaken flight

TOTEM

The owl who flies
Across the moon,
Creatures of the night
Her life-making.
From the dark ones
Sustaining her,
Throwing back bones,
Skeletons only,
The present contained,
The past discarded.
To soar,
Always the gentle
Strong beaten flight,
Wings wider than
You knew she had.
She loves to fly
And ask
Always the same,
"Are you the one?"

TELL ME TRUE

What would you like?
A poem, perhaps,
Giving you
A tiny porcelain cup
Holding the
Surging seas
Of my love for you
One syllable
Per serving.

Instead I unleash
Those tidal waves,
Covering you
With words.
More than any
Mind or heart-stream,
They submerge you.

Beneath the water
You pause,
Rejoice in the unexpected
New adventure
Before you
Bubble something
Unrelated
Then slowly float
Away.

BEST FRIENDS

We were born,
Myself and
My daughter's promise,
Twins separated
By a few years,
Nothing more.
Nevermore
The Finger wrote
On the wall
Of my womb.
Forevermore
We remain
Friends more than
Best and earnest sworn,
Shadow gift
At my birthing.

TIMID PEARLS

If you want
These words,
You have
To go deep,
Strong hands
To pull
Apart the shell
And dig
Down to the light,
Syllable
Jewels,
The ones
You want
To hide inside
Your own heart
Now.

FEATHER THOUGHTS

If I were
Really
An owl,
I'd fly
Away
Tonight
And feast
On the rat
Who runs
So fast,
Tail whipping
Sharp goodbye.

If I were
Really
So wise,
I'd fly
Over walls,
Trees,
And watch
The moon's
Many turns,
So quiet,
Silent through
Each goodbye.

But I have
No wings
Or feathers
To fly,
No taste
For the feast,
No heart-wise
For the quiet,

Only voice
For the love
And tears
For the leaving,
And nights
For remembering.

WORDS IN THE BREEZE

I am alone
I've birthed
Two shoots only
Bamboo tall
And hardening
As I sink
In this mud
Snapped and broken
Bent to the earth
Dry and brown
No softness left
Inside just
The hole
Tunnel
To the sky
And whistling
Wind talk

OLD SKIN

My skin
Is thin
And bare-
Ly holds
Me in.
Old shells
Surround
Deep sea
Within
Seen through
Salt tears
Rough swim
Through the
Hard years
My life's
Beach and
Tide gone
Out now
Dry sand
Written
Upon
Gently
Blown by
Cold wind
To rest
Where none
Knew I
Could go
Only
The clouds
Always
Reflect
Rainbows
Mirage

Of my
Ebbing
Wet heart

AFTER THIRTY-TWO YEARS

I like the bleeding
Periodicity
Mystery rituals
Touching, smelling
Taste of Earth
Drawn down
Into it
Fertility witness
With the Moon
Sworn testimony
Tides or surges
Monthly renewal of
Kali woman-vows…

GEMINI

I like to see movies
Twice,
Read favorite novels
Three times
Or five,
Breathe deeply
In and out
Every day,
Repeating the best
To suck more
Out of it
And test my perception
Of the experience,
Like husbands,
Doing them twice
Or five times,
Maybe the same one
Again a few times,
But I'm just an amateur.

Grandmother had seven
Before she quit.
We're stubborn about
Having shoes
That fit.

HILLBILLY PEDIGREE

My mother is dead
My father, too
His mother and brother before
And Mom's mom
I don't know
Where they put her
But her mind was gone
Maybe just out visiting
I think sometimes
They take these things
All too seriously
Not a smile among them
For a hundred years
Like Grandmother's sisters
All eight great-aunts
Gone on quietly
And the bastard son
Who earned his name
Lives on I've heard
Selling antiques
Or snake oil and such
And I've a brother
Or two or more
According to what I hear
When I'm listening
Too close to the door
And the aunt whose
Hypochondria is famed
In such circles
Without stop lights
Just one-lanes and paths
And the cousins who wed
The sister who's dead
The uncle who still

Climbs power poles
The older one whose
Hero mystery is unsolved
And all the unknown
The grandfathers who've come
And gone
With no smiling and no teeth
For at least
A hundred years

ASSISTED LIVING

Sometimes I think
I will never taste
A man again
And that hurts
Right down to the molars
Like tapioca when
You wanted peanut brittle
Or everyone watching
Mr. Ed when
You wanted Cary Grant
And where's the TLC
In this place anyway
I'm not feeling loved
Or very assisted

SENILITY

I have a brother
Well two really
Helps to remember
The dark side
Of the Moon
And other bodies
Skeletons really
Like the husband
Well two really
Always remembered
The tall ones
And dark
Exccpt the blonde
Who wasn't
But kept me warm
All those years
And I am cold now
Too many skeletons
No comfort in the rattle
Of those old bones
But that boy could love
My daughter had tall ones
Not dark like her daddy
She's still a miracle
I think
He was a Leo

SPIDER VEINS

I sat on my front porch
Felt rain begin to fall
On my toes, that's all.
Remembered other days
Other porches, cabins
Places to stay
Or just pass through
And the raindrops
Falling on parts of me
Left sticking out
Fingers, legs, eyelashes, shoulders
Just getting wet
Rained on
Nature-nurtured.

I felt all the years on my front porch
Stuck my legs all the way out
Rain coming down
Up to my hips
Stood up and walked about
Stuck my chin right up
Soaking hair, face, neck, dripping
Trying to figure out
How to wash my heart
Back to the beginning.

Sun popped, rain stopped
Itsy bitsy spider…

CONTRASTS

A branch
Barren stripped
Leaning down
Sharply outlined
Night time silhouette
Silent beauty
Stark statement
Whipped across the
Unsuspecting face
Bits of red flesh
Torn traces left
To soften the
Silhouette

MOTHER'S DAYS

My mother died
Never opened
Her eyes
Stubborn
To the last
Kept looking
Through the
Long nights
Swearing
There were lights
No one else
Could see
The air
My mother
Knew was there
She breathed it
Held the fear
Inside
Transmuted
When she died
The legacy
Of silence
And clay
Rock hard
Mother's way

SEVEN YEARS OLD

Sitting here so very still
Watching and watching
Ice cream melting
Running off the edge
Of the plastic tablecloth
Pink and brown and white
Napoleon Daddy calls it
His favorite
I hate strawberry
And pink dripping
On the green floor
No Christmas in July
So hot and sticky
Flies buzzing round
Making too much noise
But I'm quiet
Skinny legs so sweaty
Sticking to the vinyl
But I don't move
In July's birthday kitchen
Waiting for the beating
To end or someone to
Pass out or clean up
The ice cream
No cake this year
If I'm better
Maybe next one
With chocolate

MILK IN GLASS BOTTLES

When I was little
And I was
Postage was a nickel
And they washed your windows
At the gas station
And I thought beer
Went with potato chips
And cards
Like milk in glass bottles
At the door went with
Tuesdays and Thursdays
And poodle skirts
Went with pony tails
And we had them all
Until we grew
And the beer grew, too
And the bottles in the hall
Weren't milk anymore
And the beer got older
And vodka too
And the bottles were
Everywhere
Under the car seat
Under the bed
Under the sofa cushions
In the closet
In the bathroom
In the hole in the wall
And they moved
Sometimes through the air
Thrown in rage
No target wide enough
No child small enough
The stakes were higher

And the postage went up
Too

CHILDREN IN TRANSITION

Too much rough stuff here
Punching and kicking
Throwing kids against the wall
Slapping switches belts
And shoes
Those shoes
Anything convenient
Fists will do
Or buckles
To beat the juice out
Blood or joy
Doesn't matter
Kill the living
But don't tell
Don't breathe a word
Don't breathe
At all

THE PIT AND THE PENDULOUS

There is a pit
Inside a woman
That anatomy ignores
And physicians never probe,
A pit dug out
By every word and stare,
Offhand comment handed out:
Legs and hips,
Noses, breasts too large
Too small, too high,
Too low, too fast,
Too slow, too round,
Too long, too short.
Nature deals in "too's" for us:
Too this, too that.
And the pit grows.
It grows and grows.
And, God, too often
It shows, it shows.
And we live with restrictions,
Boundaries to being
Set by the terrible "too's":
Too fat for this,
Too skinny for that,
Too fair, too dark,
Too long, too short,
Too round, too flat.
Our pendulum swings, sharper, sharper.
Everyday we fight it, fight it.
Too old, too old, to live, to live.
Too young, too young, to die, to die
And escape the pit at last.

BELLY BUTTON

"Suck it in,"
The mother said,
"Don't show
Your gut."
The boy stopped
Breathing,
Improvising,
Acquiescent,
As his smile,
His heart,
Died,
Frozen,
Fixed
On a navel.
Umbilical
Piercing.

WOMEN'S WAYS

Grandmother started
Dying
They left her
In the yard
Hot day
Wash on the line
Convened
A committee
To decide
What to do
Perhaps.

Sister died
Before
She was born
Buried at night
Aunt Blanche died
Fell off the bed
Or jumped
Only babies
Wiser than
The rest
Perhaps.

Mother stayed so
Father beat her
Brother too
Till she died
Sylvia put her
Head in an oven
It is rumored
She died too
Impressed with
The Pit
Perhaps.

FATHER'S DAYS

When you told me
B's weren't good enough
But grades weren't
Important anyway
For girls and
How I was too
Smart for any
Man who'd want
To have me
Any
Way
I believed you.

When you hit me
Held me down
Covered my mouth
Told me not
To breathe a word
They'd think I was
Crazy and
Nothing happened
Any
Way
I believed you.

When you drank and
Smoked and
Popped pills and
Told me
You could quit
Any
Time
And I asked
You to please now

And you said
Sure baby doll
I believed you.

Like I did when
You said you were
Gonna' die and
I left the university
And you didn't
Then
Any
Way.

And you died later
Instead
Face down in
Your own vomit
Alone
But you came
By my house
First
See-through
Light-style
Just to tell me
You were sick and
Sorry and
Once more
I believed you.

WHEN WE WERE CARDS

Faces sad, long, frowning
Sketched in carefully coded keypunched cards
Through the holes in them
When viewed in the light
Sorrow punched in along with
Directions to the contrary
"Do not fold, spindle, mutilate"
Scarred by the instruction
To avoid damaging individuation
Perforated lines drawn in for
Eyes, mouth, lashes, ears
Paper faces crinkle, wrinkle
More quickly than wash-and-wear
Cardboard lips touching, bending
Say, "Do not fold or tear"
The conformity of our lives
Checked, validated, duplicated
And put in boxes
Made to fit
In the end

CONSCIOUSNESS-RAISING
ON THE GRASS

a three-legged dog
someone saw and directed
eyes and faces toward
oh and ahh and how
sad and watch
he must envy the other
wild dogs running
barking but how quickly
he moves how well
he has adapted to
his condition missing
one leg severed neatly
almost natural it seems
but the complex he must
have frustration with
three legs only but
how well he runs
with normal dogs
he's not like other three
legged dogs at all I
think I might like him

WOODSTOCK AFTER KENT

His name was Woodstock
I don't know why
He'd never been there
But everyone loved him
Because he wasn't quiet
Or quite like
Any other cat
We'd ever known
And he was a lot
Like us, I guess
Not quiet and
Not like any people
We'd ever known
Either
And we lived together
And were happy
Until one of the people
We'd never known
Not like us
Decided that cats
Should all be alike
And quiet
And decided that
Woodstock wasn't
And decided to remedy
That situation
And we found our friend
Dead
That morning

LIBERATION

I heard my unborn daughter
Crying for her freedom,
Crying for her life
Instead of darkness.

And I went out to make a revolution
That her daughter might be free.

EVENINGS AT HOME

you get to be
obsessive living
alone I've heard
friends say I
have to agree
I make myself
laugh at jokes
out loud when
I'm alone just
so I don't forget
how to in case
I'm ever not
the uncertainty of
it all bugs me
and I am trying
not to laugh now
but I like bells
chimes music TV
anything that sounds
when I'm not
I like to hear the
furnace work to
make me warm

RUNNING AGAIN

You may go
Now
Or then
But it will
Not end
Not now
Not later.
I watch
Your journey.
You love
The drive.
You make up
Maps
Along the way.
The rolling is
The pleasure.
Crank it up.
Start
The engine
Again.

POLITE EX'S

We talk tight,
Words layered
Like lace
Of cobwebs,
Sticky stuff
That goes with you
In pieces.
The spiders
Bite later.

CAVE THOUGHTS

I am empty,
A deep, woman's emptiness.
The loss of men –
Father, husband, son.

Men are lost.
Why is it that the way?
Women are severed,
One from the other.
We disconnect, move apart.

We lose fathers, husbands, sons.
The poisons take them, shape them,
Bury them in a stranger's plot.
The toil and sweat and glory of it all
Make them lose their way home
As often as not,
And they are lost,
To children, wives, mothers, lovers.

Women need knives, blades, the sharpness
To come between us.
Miles, rails, mountains, wings will suffice.
Words will often do the trick, too.
With purpose we nurture, make, bake
Our hearts' interweaving.
Then with intent we cut the strings
To fly free, begin elsewhere,
Watch pieces fall.

But men we just lose,
One after another,
The holding together
Too mysterious,

Too uncertain,
To fully comprehend.
The horizons they march to
Too rigid to bend,
Too far a journey
To ever truly end.
We just lose them.

BENJAMIN F.

Check's in the mail
All I get
Voice mail
E-mail
Check's in it
All male
Remote control
Even now
Damned engineer
Screwed electronically
Digitally
Without the satisfaction
Of long-lasting batteries
Or pink bunny

TOKENISM

I made it in their world,
Achieving my quota of ulcers and Tums
At a remarkably youthful age.
Iron gates creaked open at my attack,
Revealing iron rooms and residents within.
And, as I stormed the last bastion, I asked,
"Where is the victory?"
Loudly treading down halls of metal,
Puzzlement grew at the lack of defense,
And I asked, "Where are the guardians?"
On past silent metal-men I climbed,
Never detecting the expected steps behind.
The heights scaled finally,
The door thrust open to reveal
Iron men in an iron prison
Seen through hardened metallic orbs.
Where is the victory, indeed?

INITIATION

I saw a baby today
    in a trash can.
Her mother must have though it a fresh
    and revolutionary method of orientation
    for new-born ignorance
To be exposed to the vital stuff of life
    early
So as to avoid disappointment
    in later weeks and months
    and years and decades
    of exposure
To even bigger trash
    and garbage
    and other basic facts of life
Her mother had learned
    so well.

THE MARRIED MAN

In the end
When you spoke
Of the surprise
You could not give
Me a thing
But words and words
"Love, love, love"
For two, you guessed
And more, I'm sure
And apologies, regrets
For wanting me
Inside you and
Not having me
And building swimming pools
Gazebos, second mortgages
Old people going on
Cruises together
Alone with secrets, and
Happier, I am sure
Forty years together
With the shadow
Me inside you
Always clawing
Gnawing, knowing
I rage through you
Tearing, biting, caged
Unsuspecting implant
Inside a heart that
Could love, could give
But took, forsook
Leaving me lost
Inside you somewhere
Traveling veins, capillaries
Aorta, ventricles

Pumping, pumping
Always there, you
Not knowing where or
When I bite, pull
You back to that night
And lovers' hearts
Exploding with the merge
Two welded but disintegrating
Straightening faces, roles
Exits with the pieces
Of each other planted
Left atrium, ready
To share a secret
With every vein
Always bringing back the pain
All we had to give

EPILOGUE

act III finale
curtain coming down
one encore
then another
and they're gone
house lights flash on
everyone's leaving
faces scrambling into aisles
and on out into the street
off with my costume
naked once again
the makeup comes slowly
painted smile peeling off
only the woman
and mirror
once again
out into the cold
deserted darkened downtown
no longer the actress
reciting my lines
away from the lover role
and back to tiny
fourth floor apartment
and more fantasy love plays
with tea stains within
cold and lonely again
another script tomorrow
like Romeo lover tonight
memorizing familiar scenes
and moving on
to one more stage
and one more balcony
and another star
like you

FANTASIES

I wish the dreams were enough,
The deepest of fantasies,
Passionate stuff.
But dreams cannot fill me,
Cannot warm me,
Truly hold me,
Walk with me.

And dreams are, after all,
Too likely to become aspirations,
Beginnings of plans.
Lost dreams merely bring wistfulness.
Broken plans make holes, tears,
In hearts and minds.
The fabric is stronger
Unmended.

BREAKUP INSOMNIA

Waiting for the magic dream phase
To be initiated, phased in, switched on.
For pills to give thrills or the lack of them,
To prompt the sun or hasten the stars.
Waiting for you, my love, to cry,
To understand hunger without bread,
Thirst in an endless desert.
Waking each day without you,
Waiting for the peace to begin.
The joy I falsely offer to outstretched hands,
Never telling of nights stolen,
Thievery of their unspoken optimism,
The peace their eyes say they hope I have,
Created, offered, taken,
But never held within me.
Waiting until I'm alone again,
Knowing I've always been, even with you.
Wondering if I'll always be.
Hoping, somehow, you're lonely, too.
Cringing at the bitterness that remains,
Frightened that nightmares still empty into sleep
All the debris from our demolition.
Waiting for the good times, the magic,
Pausing with Merlin capsules now.

FOREVER FLOWERS

A lover, presenting
Flowers delicate
Petals perfect
Pistils sterile
No pollen, no sneezing
Copper-colored perfection
Promising eternity
Wilt-less, flawless
Copper wire shaped slyly
To resemble daisies, daffodils
Roses, rhododendron
Copper flowers from my lover
Lasting forever, unchanging
Permanence gained at the cost
Of artificiality

DOMESTICITY

Sweet singing birds,
Two doves in one nest.
Pages from old newspapers, magazines
And fiction – a canary found
At the bottom
Of her mate's cage,
Quite quiet at last,
Her feathers plucked, bleeding.
Quite quiet, quite, quite dead.
I swing, I swing,
Waiting.

ABOUT THE AUTHOR

Lin Forest was born in the foothills of the Smokey Mountains and lived there until she began her wandering, living in more than 25 different homes in the past 30 years. Her working life has included the roles of writer, editor, teacher, computer consultant, sociologist, marketing director and law firm administrator. "I dance with life," she says, "and I like to learn new steps!"

Lin has married, divorced, raised children and says that she now lives as a "hermit-crab". One of her greatest delights is to create inspirational experiences for others to share what she has experienced in her life's journey. "A smile, a wink, a laugh, a sigh and a tear are all good things to share," she says. "You have to laugh."

www.ingramcontent.com/pod-product-compliance
Lightning Source LLC
Chambersburg PA
CBHW031255060726
47590CB00003B/924